LOVE'S INSTRUMENTS

MELVIN DIXON

WITH AN
INTRODUCTION BY
ELIZABETH ALEXANDER

TIA CHUCHA PRESS
CHICAGO

ACKNOWLEDGMENTS

Thanks to the editors of the following publications in which many of these poems first appeared, some in slightly different form:

Beloit Poetry Journal: "Chill"

Black American Literature Forum: "Obsidian," "Silent Reaper"

Black World: "Wood and Rain"

Callaloo: "The Alchemist's Dilemma," "Place, Places"

Hollow Springs Poetry Review: "Paring Potatoes"

In the Life: A Black Gay Anthology: "Etymology," "Getting Your Rocks Off"

The Kenyon Review: "And These Are Just A Few"

Mouth of the Dragon: "Autumn Leaving," "Wednesday Mourning," "The Man from Bombay"

New York Native: "Keeping Time"

Obsidian: "Celebration"

Ploughshares: "Aunt Ida Pieces a Quilt," "Into Camp Ground"

Poets for Life: 76 Poets Respond to AIDS: "The 80s Miracle Diet," "Heartbeats," "One by One"

Presence Africaine: "Veve in Haiti"

Southern Review: "After Prayers at Twilight," "Altitudes," "Hands," "Mother's Tour," "Winter Gardens," "Winter Without Snow"

Thanks also to the Research Foundation of the City University of New York, The National Endowment for the Arts and the Lannan Foundation for grants to complete and publish this book.

Robert Giard's photograph of Melvin Dixon comes from his project "Particular Voices: Portraits of Gay and Lesbian Writers." He has photographed over 500 writers, and the project is ongoing. Giard writes: "Photography is par excellence the medium of our mortality, holding up, as it does, one time for the contemplation of another time. This motif infuses all portraiture with a special poignancy. It is my wish that tomorrow, when a viewer looks into the eyes of the subjects of these portraits, she/he will say in a spirit of wonder, 'These people were here; they lived and breathed.' So too will the portraits respond, 'We were here; we existed. This is how we were.'"

ISBN 1-882688-07-4
Library of Congress Catalog Card Number: 95-68621

Book Design: Jane Brunette Kremsreiter
Cover Painting: Untitled, 1991, Christopher Dixon
Back cover photo: Robert Giard

PUBLISHED BY:
TIA CHUCHA PRESS
A Project of the Guild Complex
PO Box 476969
Chicago, IL 60647

DISTRIBUTED BY:
NORTHWESTERN UNIVERSITY PRESS
Chicago Distribution Center
11030 S. Langley
Chicago, IL 60628
phone: 1-800-621-2736
fax: 1-800-621-8476

CONTENTS

Introduction :: 5

H A N D S

S K I N   T O   S K I N

H E A R T B E A T S

INTRODUCTION

Tia Chucha Press is proud to publish *Love's Instruments*, this last collection of poems by Melvin Dixon. Dixon died on October 26, 1992, of an AIDS-related illness; the poems in this book are powerful enough without that piece of biography, but they accrue further meaning in the context both of literature of this plague and the premature loss of their author.

AIDS has, of course, defined and devastated our times, and the ranks of artists and people of color have been particularly decimated. When literary historians try to write the story of gay black poetry in the late twentieth century, it will be a history swathed with absence. There are the absent dead whose books are left behind as well as those whose works only remain in anthologies, or perhaps in notebooks hidden from the rest of the world. And there are those who fell silent as they devoted their physical and psychic energies to struggling with disease. But as the background of a painting shapes its composition, absence can also be understood as presence. We can see and hear and read absence as a presence that profoundly marks the cultural history of our times.

Melvin Dixon was prodigiously accomplished in his 42 years. He grew up in Stamford, Connecticut, and received his B.A. from Wesleyan University in 1971 and then doctorate from Brown University in 1975. Throughout his career he travelled the world, spending large amounts of time especially in Dakar, Senegal, and Paris, France. He won many grants including a French Government Fellowship, a Ford Foundation Postdoctoral Fellowship, and a Scholar-in-Residence Fellowship from the Schomburg Center for Research in Black Culture. He taught at Williams College, Fordham, and Columbia University, and for the last part of his teaching career was Professor of English at Queen College and the Graduate Center of the City University of New York.

Dixon wrote in many different genres: *Change of Territory* (poems), *Trouble the Waters* and *Vanishing Rooms* (novels), and *Ride Out the Wilderness: Geography and Identity in Afro-American Literature* (literary criticism). He translated Geneviève Fabre's study of African-American drama, *Drumbeats, Masks, and Metaphors*, as well as the mammoth, definitive translation of the complete poems of the Senegalese poet Leopold Sedar Senghor. He was a writer and a scholar who refused to draw hard and fast distinctions between the activities of the sides of the brain. He called himself "a person of letters" whose religion was writing, whatever form it took.

Many poets have written poems in dedication to Dixon, a testament to the lasting, inspirational legacy of his work. Cyrus Cassell's "Marathon," Patricia Smith's "The Touching of Him," Marilyn Hacker's "Against Elegies," John Keene's "Echoes That Come," and my own "Dream" and "At the Beach" are dedicated to Melvin Dixon. Few writers as young receive such tribute from their peers.

Dixon's poems are elegant and suffused with integrity, humor, and erudition. He knew and had seen a lot, and this varied knowledge is very much evident in the poems. *Love's Instruments* concludes with Dixon's speech given at the 1992 OutWrite conference for Gay and Lesbian writing in Boston. It stands as one of the most important essays written about writing in the age of AIDS, and it offers an example of Dixon's prose eloquence, as well as his fierce intellectual and political commitment to the many issues raised by the disease's rampage through our society.

Cyrus Cassell's "Marathon" aptly describes Melvin Dixon's "sensuous and hilarious wit." Melvin was my friend and mentor for many years; I would characterize him as most essentially possessing fierce elegance, the fiercest, not a decorative elegance but rather a distilled and streamlined way of being and presenting. Or, in the vernacular, Melvin was *fierce*. Since we know he is supervising this project from his fabulous throne in the firmament, we hope and believe that he will be pleased with the way *Love's Instruments* has turned out. When Melvin died this book was not placed with Tia

Chucha Press, so we have tried our best to make the book one he would be proud of. We have left the manuscript in the order in which he arranged it and added this introduction and the OutWrite speech as an afterward. We also chose the cover painting, which was done by Melvin's brother, Christopher Dixon. Tragedy sometimes shamelessly compounds itself; Christopher also died of AIDS. This book, then, is a testament as well to his beauty, brilliance, and talent.

Melvin has left us with a richly learned, insightful, stirring body of work. He has also left us with a lot of work to do ourselves as we proceed with our own projects and carrying on the work of brothers and sisters exited far too soon. In "Against Elegies," Marilyn Hacker writes that she hopes those who have left will know "I used their names/as flares in a polluted atmosphere." At OutWrite, Melvin Dixon said: "You, then, are charged by the possibility of your good health, by the broadness of your vision, to remember us."

. . . . .

Deepest thanks to the Dixon family, particularly Melvin's mother, Jessie Dixon, and his sister, Deanna Dixon, for their invaluable support of the publication of this book. Thanks to Barbara Bowen, Faith Hampton Childs, Cyrus Cassells, and Robert Giard, and special gratitude to Marcellus Blount, diligent and loving sustainer of Melvin's work. Finally, Melvin wrote these poems with the love and support of his life partner, Richard A. Horovitz, who died of AIDS in July 1991.

Elizabeth Alexander
University of Chicago

■ ■ ■

Oh, master now love's instruments—
complex and not for the fearful,
simple and not for the foolish.
Master now love's instruments.

I who love you tell you this,
even as the pitiful killer waits for me,
I who love you tell you this.

ROBERT HAYDEN
"WORDS IN THE MOURNING TIME"

■ ■ ■

It ain't right, that sortta thing.
What thing?
Just don't come back here.
Me or him, Daddy?
It don't make me no difference.

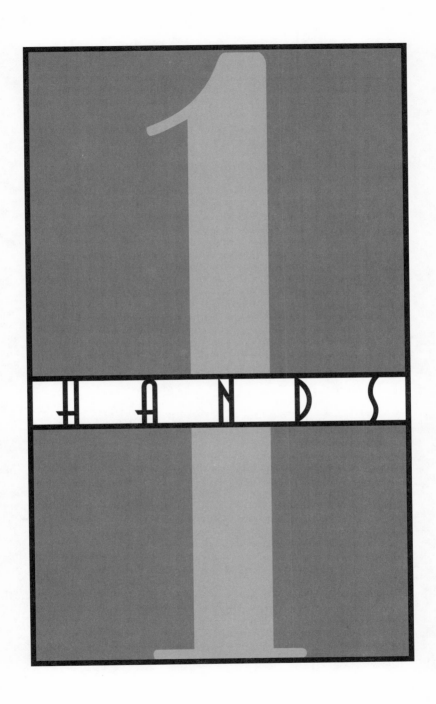

HANDS

PARING POTATOES

I take two from the sack,
examine their round dust bottoms
where something else has eaten
between the pipes and onions.

Roaches dig there, leaving skin
and hollow vegetable.
From one starchy tunnel
a root hangs limp. My hands

rest at the spot, a knife
ready for the food
one man can find.

In this kitchen space of two men
and brown bottom
tunnels of roaches and quick hunger
something else eats here the bleeding

pulp, the vitamin juice gone
in the crunch of roach wings,
and gouged eyes clinging
from the empty food.
My stomach eats itself hollow

like a gourd in winter
as potato eyes
rimmed with mold
watch my black paring hands.

C H I L L

Mosquitoes in August,
then September flies swarm inside.
They've come to savor dinner scraps
and the cartilage of raw ears.

Caught fat and full at the screen
they smash drunk, bulbous eyes
looking out. Their wings whine
against the enemy of wire
as your skin pulls tight.

You bathe, then shiver for sleep.
Birch branches claw at the window,
reach for you, yellow and curl
at the touch of glass or skin.

Morning you find the lingering
breath of nightmare on every mirror
and outside
where sparrows angle away
and don't look back.

O B S I D I A N

FOR ALVIN AUBERT

Volcanic glass. Smokey shards
primed and polished. I spew
from the raging earth
in all directions. Chilled
and crystallized, I can become
religious ornaments in Arizona,
arrowheads old men call
Apache tears, or simply
the cutting
black edge of a knife.

MAN HOLDING BOY

AFTER A PHOTOGRAPH BY JOHN WHITE

Hunched forward under rain
like liquid steel upon his skin
he pushes ahead. The boy
locked to his chest, asleep.

He weighs this storm. His eyes
no longer begging clouds for comfort,
but testing the ground and the boy
still safe beneath his shoulders.

Rain spikes beating the old head
silence
once the boy awakes.
There are no more songs but his stirring.

HANDS

Once teaching English in Ivory Coast
you gave the ritual handshake all around
and someone teased the texture of your palms:
"*Mais Monsieur, vous n'avez jamais
cultivé la terre.*" And not until
walking the road from Tiebissou,
laterite caking the skin, did you
contemplate the rain-forgotten soil
or the emptiness of your hands.

When we met on the abused asphalt
of Sheridan Square, our hands lost altitude,
our eyes gripped hungrily to eyes.
I said, "I'm Handy's boy."
Already touched and tattooed. My blood
is southern laterite, my cradle
Connecticut, and my skin
the color you've kissed before.

Once rhyming English in Massachusetts,
teaching metaphor and meter, I heard
the veiled dissension: "But Sir,
you have never worked the land."
Yet even then, trailing the Berkshires,
my legs brittle twigs among the trees,
did my fingers cup on pine cones
and the fixed solitude of winter.

Here in the fist of New York City
elbowing the Atlantic, or in Dakar,
jagged peninsula begging the geography,

these instruments of embrace between us
reach and reel and roll and reap—
these calluses are none but our own.

SPRING CLEANING

First goes floordust, then newspapers
stacked near the bed. Peanut shells
swept out of hiding between mattress
and rug. Toenails clipped.
Sprouts of a beard shaved off.
With hourly glasses of Deer Park Water
and the barest of food, the body
sheds winter fat and filler.

The hair goes next, close
to the gleaming, gleaming skull.
You are ready for the sun
and the salt-tongued air.

You are someone new. I will be
someone new, like you, and promise
not to hear the rattle our bones make
moving from empty closets
and all through the room.

GETTING YOUR ROCKS OFF

Reading clouds beyond the road
I calculate our distance, survey
the space between our clothes
where rising curves and mountain
tug for air, touch, release.

You drive to the hairpin slope,
hesitate, turn up and in. We ride
on every naked fear you have
and discover that men like us
are not all granite, shale,
deceptive quartz, or
glittering layers of mica.

From here you see the whole world
differently: brownskin,
tufts of black grass.
And many times I have given myself
to summits like these.
Ride in, ride high.
Ride until the clouds break.

You will learn to read rain. You will
follow the white gravel it leaves.

WOOD AND RAIN

PARIS, BOIS DE BOULOGNE

I am black man of woods
weeping
where trees
root like men
hollering in the wind
for lost children,

where folds of knotted skin
break off
and stab the ground, and fat
black fingers
sky-scratch a warning:

there is no hiding, there is no home
in wet woods or this soil.

Here a leaf drops
like a dead bird.
Listen, the woods weep.
My fingers grip the dirt where I fall.

MOTHER'S TOUR

At the Louvre you find Mona Lisa
gone secretly to Japan, Egyptian mummies
closed, Greek statues so arresting
and erect that you stumble. I catch you
falling, but not the pain rising inside.
Hours later you can't walk. I translate
in Emergency, broken foot? sprained ankle?

As the swelling eases you limp
to where my friend and I have slept.
Sightseeing us naked and embraced and chiseled
in surprise breaks what your pills and gauze
held tight, sends us packing separate souvenirs:
his razor, my guidebooks, your figurines
cracked from travels swelling our distance.

K E E P I N G   T I M E

This night so gently
we circle the clock of streets.
I hear your feet before we meet,
I've come empty like this before.
My mouth parched on "hello"
fracturing me inside, my eyes
blurring like seaglass
at other faces you've shown.

So come with me again.
What we call ourselves they have
no names for, nor the peeled

fruit offered between us.
And with lips round in even
cadence, we shall recall
this night so gently.

P O S S E S S I O N

Brown lips and fingers
limp sex and toes
float in the open jar.
You hold my parts
more calmly than before.
Your reflection
settles with such ease
upon the glass.
Your sighs of relief
bubble at the surfaces
of skin then vanish
as my swelling pores
whisper,
"We got you. We got you."

26

ETYMOLOGY:
A FATHER'S GIFT

He surveys our gathering. He
searches the dictionary for clues
to what we say we want. His silence
hides the correct pronunciation,
the power of consonants, the meaning
he's found in words such as beg:

"To ask for as charity, to ask
a favor, to ask earnestly, entreat.
To insist in asking for something
to which one has no claim or right."

The youngest daughter coaxes him
with a kiss, her lips returning empty.
The elder girl with the soft curl of dance.
My mother with hair in premature gray
and nervous fingers caressing space.
The first son with a long jazz solo.
The third boy and I, at any stranger's crotch,
with a stuttering stuttering for the root.

DANCE FOR FATHER

FOR CYNTHIA

Seven-year-old in broken tap dance,
black hair sweated thin, legs long,
fists balled up brown and tight,
her face cut in old woman lines
screaming

> *"Daddy do something.*
> *Do something Daddy, please."*

Her lips quivering and wet,
her ass blood-hot with rash,
the medicine not working
the doctor not in

> *"Daddy do something.*
> *Do something Daddy, please."*

He held her. He cried.

SKIN TO SKIN

WINTER GARDENS

In the garden of the Tuileries
men move stiffly through the cold,

their eyes freeze on one anothers'
until the grating screech of lens

on lens, irregular sparks
of gravel against gravel,

skin to skin.

Their feet chart the ground
in the different language I read.

The signs repeat in Central Park,
Golden Gate, or Lake Shore Drive,

and I'm the New World hunter
circling, circling back.

All our footprints lead the same.

BREAKING TAP DANCE

Black gods in a tap dance
ain't no soft-shoe blues.
The first poetry is conjure,
words moving feet like angry lips.

Black god in exile
is a running, running blood root.
Dance, nigger, dance.
Second set: feet shooting.

*forced to dance — is
there still joy in the act?
Violence in dance.*

SILENT REAPER

FOR CHARLES H. ROWELL

I have been in the fields all day.
—Jean Toomer

Telephone cables are the crops of technology
above your garden of rich Kentucky loam.
The gridwork on the ground—rows of melons
and marigolds, the shock of pole beans,
Kentucky Wonders—clings madly
from vine to vine. In parallel graph
our wires grow thick with words of comfort,
your fruit aching for the harvest pluck.

No matter how safely you sink the seeds
or scarecrow them into bloom, loneliness
sprouts up quick as ragweed, choking
the collards and okra we need
for a callaloo cuisine.

In the best of gardens anything can happen:
tendrils and talk and the touch of hands
working rows of promises. You weed
and cultivate. No wonder
you are back-sore and weary—
a single hoe clawing for food
and for the simple geometry of grace.

Winter
garden
p 31

Ships open my dark thighs
as day dies slowly from disease.
Moonlight probes my earth vulva,
empty and dry until the beams
shoot through. Tides curl my sex-soft
grassy hair, cradle a howling
from the sea, trill rat feet
scattering each blade. And I
create history once again
from this coffin length of space,
this steady rocking upon the waves.

A F T E R P R A Y E R S
A T T W I L I G H T

DAKAR, SENEGAL

Pirogues in silhouettes on the sea,
fishermen hauling their catch
up the hub of beach brick, harmattan dust
in their hair and everywhere. Night tilts
this dry cup of the continent.
I, too, came from the sky. You can't see
my footprints anymore. Look there,
quickly, the spilled calabash of sunset.
Burnt air clinging to my clothes.
Now can you see them?
Crescent toes, brown stars.

AFRICAN BEACH SCENE

ST. LOUIS, SENEGAL

Black boys running into the sea
are wave hunters.
Black men sleeping at noon
are dream fisherman.
Tides breaking on the shore
leave older footprints.

Veve IN HAITI

voodoo loa
—rep. during
ritual

FOR JACQUES BRIERRE

after the dance each line
blows back to skies fed on
drum lines lived on earth and
danced from corn flour sifted
into face flat circles
brown with seeds for eyes
that look from root hairs
guiding feet frenzied
into dance when after the dance
lines shape the wind
possessed of life.

Feathered head gripped
in tree tough hands
whirls through a time
it owned
before *crack* and *snap*
send wings and body
flapping into death
possessed by brown
lady fingers.
White feathers
at her drumming feet
settle into *vévés* of war
on the bloody ground
where a rooster
pecks nervously
at scattered
corn.

THE ALCHEMIST'S DILEMMA

1. Ebony and Sand

Mohammed of the *Cour des maures*
sells silver bracelets, ebony rings,
and coffers left by groaning caravans.
Prices drift from sand between his teeth.
His camel-fitted torso so close
I can nuzzle grains of the Sahara
in his robes. But beware.

It is water he needs. A currency
more magical than gold, more slippery
than commerce through his hands
cracked open like the soil.

Water. He can smell it on my skin.
Rain so scant teenagers in Mauritania
dream it is cooler than the copper hills.
Will it clean arms and toes
for *"Allah Akbar. Allah Akbar?"*
If there's no water, use sand.

Brown faces among the black,
flecks of another country in Dakar.
Mohammed of the *Cour des maures.*
strides the night in Arabic,
calling as many names for sand
as Eskimos have for snow.

Climb the dunes of cloth about his waist.
See if you can pry the evening prayer
from his lips onto yours.

2. Ebony and Silver

Workshop coals heat tools and tea.
We suck three frothy rounds
high up the throat, each swallow
on the benediction *"Alhamdoulilai."*
Mohammed pumps the goatskin bellows,
takes up ebony at the grain.

He files, then shaves, gouges tracks
in wood like the hooves of camels.
Imbeds silver so it glistens,
the only galaxy navigating the desert.
Ebony clings to silver, silver fuses in wood.
This alchemy in Africa is older than we know.
Which gives value to which?
The alchemist's dilemma. Our prize.

3. Ebony and Cotton

Moustapha of the *Cite des Artistes*
weds fabric to cardboard in figures of dance.
From Dutch wax, raffia, mud cloth of Niger
suddenly *griots* and granaries take shape.
Faces lost in market mazes
come back to be fixed under glass.

Except first wife and child dead
before his house was finished, or bricks
longing for the kiss of water and cement—
silhouettes in the collage he lives.

His aging father told him:
Feel for the raw grain as you build
and the cloth you cut will protect from pain.
Yet Moustapha awoke in the hospital ward
screaming so deeply no one could hear him.

His voice came back, but not his ears.
He started painting with fabric
to hear faces speak from his hands.
Black ovals with razor eyes, woven lips
singing to watercolor skies, red string
kora and fish net catch Moustapha
of the *Cite des Artistes* without a cure.

4. Ebony and Me

How to transmute metals into gold?
Mix languages. Let metaphor ferment.
How to draw water from dry rock?
Trade smiles, not discounts.
How to cure disease, prolong life?
Feed the dead with songs and sweat.

The alchemist's dilemma?
Perhaps only mine.

One night Mohammed in jeans and T-shirt
and I wearing sandals and robes
walked arm in arm through Dakar
where men can do such things.
From the most grainy embrace of our
ebony and clothes and sand his fingers
fled, leaving in every groove of me
this raging glimmer of silver.

CAMBRAI: EXIT VISA

FOR DIDIER

At four years old
you visit neighboring farms,
read the newspaper
as they vaccinate cattle.

Later by the fireside
you read aloud and count
to one hundred as they listen:
proud parents who know
the cure of animals,
amused farmers
settling their account.

They ask what you'd like to become.
Their eyes fix on the print of war
and industry. Your child voice
anxious, alert: "An American!"
forgetting faces there that look
from one to one
and nervously laugh.

EXCEPT FOR SAND

No news from France tonight
except for memory in the dark,
what swells and pulls
for liquid taste with the rush
and break of Mediterranean waves.

The sand at sunset cooled us
tight together. We shook with August
evening chill, and stains
like fat raindrops marked our place.
We ran home before the tide
swallowed our footprints

As if there would be no news from here
except for sand scratching inside bent shoes
or spilling from corners of the eyes.

APARTMENT FOR RENT:
Rue de l'Amiral-Mouchez, Paris

We don't want no
colored people
here either.

WINTER WITHOUT SNOW

Harmattan starts its December howling,
hurling grit of the Sahara all around.
Don't look to the sky for rescue.
Breathe, and you fill up with sand.

Run to the woods and the grass has dried.
Those baobab trees are the squat arms
of grandfathers poking from their graves,
some hands waving us out to play, some
holding back the brown fog from the blue.

It's no trick, no delicate mirage.
Screech like a hawk when your feet won't move,
nobody hears you, and roaches big as thumbs
come crumbing at your toes, the ants to dance.
Stay where you are, grow round and down.

Remember your father's cough, the hacking phlegm,
your uncle's South brown teeth? Ever wonder
why fingers crook where they come from?
It's your turn to sun burn. Just don't let them
catch you combing desert dust from your hair.

GRANDMOTHER:
CROSSING JORDAN

Rippling hospital sheets
circle your brown body
and you sink
for the third time,
ready to rise alone
on the other side.

I reach out for you
and pull and pull
until your skin tears
from the bones of elbow,
arm, wrist, and fingers.

How it hangs empty,
loose. A glove
too large
for my hand.

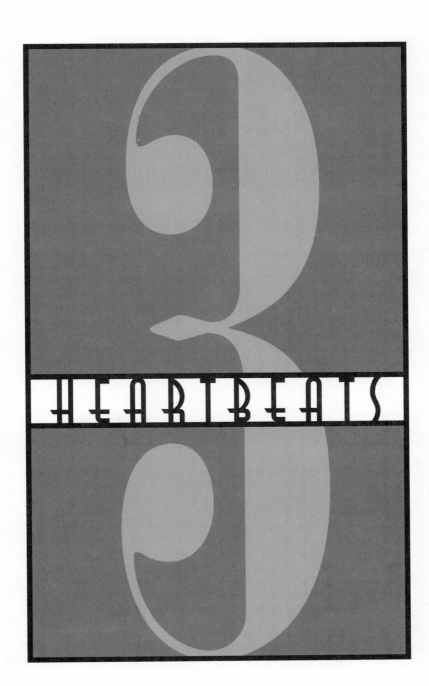

HEARTBEATS

AUTUMN LEAVING

FOR DIDIER

Vermont leaves under glass,
Your hands working the frame.
Each piece of tree and trail
For an easy reference.

Like the leaf whose red
Held fast for years
By your touch. Like me?

Black as bark, my grainy
Knuckles about to bud.
And on me everywhere
The print of fingers.

My chest become maple,
Thighs branched in two directions
From one lean trunk, one
Swollen searching taproot.

Here without you I prune myself
Repeatedly,

My hands pulling for seeds
Over the paths you took to leave:
Before, behind, and in.

Leaf after leaf of skin
Peels off.
Have you forgotten these?

THE MAN FROM BOMBAY

1.

He knows the breaking
in my years; my eyes have
the ash look he has seen before,
my body the smell of age, mildew.

Mystic, he calls himself.
"But don t be afraid.
I have a message for you.
Please, don't be afraid."

I say I'm leaving. I'll take
my dying somewhere else
with empty brain and thighs
bruised from strangers pumping there.

"I know you like the young stuff,"
he says. "But come anyway. You'll find
it's not the young who give
but those who have learned it,
those who have lived."

I warn that I take sweat
like some men take blood. And blood
like men take sweat. He leads
fearlessly to the liquid testing.
Mystic, he says again,
his limp foot touching mine.

2.
His lips circle and wet.
The fill of blood leaves me
hungry. Sweat at corners of his mouth
beads like short tears, softens
tongue, teeth and words

glued in the throat
like the prayers of pilgrims.
Streams inside me seal the cry.
My hands slip from his secret skin.
What water is this
cleaning me before I drown?

3.
Age swallows age. The room breathes.
Lips search the dark. One eye
swims into another.

Then alone I pull on his pants
for bandage.

And where limp steps dissolved
acidly,
the night calls after me
to stay.

PLACE, PLACES

The first night you were gone
I heard fingers clawing from the closet
walls. Some mouse maybe, some
thing was caught between stud beams
and plaster. All next day
it tried to dig through, to nest
in your sheets and blankets
tiny paws, teeth, and nose
in a desperate bid for air.

Then all was quiet.
I looked for the gnawed exit,
the footprints, any other signs
of quick release, but nothing found.
Slowly filling from room to room
was the smell of dead flesh and fur.
I opened every window against
the silence and the odorous fusion
of bones into the architecture.

I cleaned the closet anyway,
emptied trash, washed dishes
I had dirtied all alone, remade
the bed with each corner in tight.
Here in full view is a place for me
again. You come home hungry, tired.

And I return from a different journey,
my hands stirring the air, air.

W E D N E S D A Y   M O U R N I N G

prayer

Ohio State murders

Morning blood on my pillow,
dried brown from the night fighting me
and I don't know why.

I check myself and find no cuts,
no pimples scratched off, no teeth
loose and gummy, no fingers peeled,

but lips swollen from calling his name
and feeling my head and throat run dry—
the fluids fled are body tears
that take their mourning weight.

My head empties after drink or dream.
But this is not the first blood—two,
three, four mornings straight,
in different pillow spots when I awake

and coloring my whole day red.
My eyes tell it: someone
upstairs inside me is dying
not the first death.

different symptom of AIDS - loss of lover - grief - manifests itself physical

O C T O B E R   P A S S I N G

Burnt leaves are the season's footsteps
marching in. Yellows and reds still clinging
at the root shape like the hands of children
not yet ready, not yet strong, but burning

so invisibly. October sheds the green flesh year.
This is no easy season change, no easy fire.
And the miles of smoke that separate us
screaming here still cover historic ground.

ALTITUDES

FOR RICHARD: CENTRIPETAL, EARTH SIGN

1.
It was memory that had me. Memory
with a smile and two feet, olive skin
and Gauloise on the breath saying
"bonjour" and asking my name and
waiting for the quick free fall.

I wanted the live vowels of that tongue
opening like legs and lips in love
back in 1973. So I stalked the old
neighborhood in this City of Lights
where I come from any place dark: Martinique,
Guadeloupe, Haiti, and yes, Harlem, sometimes.

"Pourqoui tu parles si bien le français?"

His names were different, but the ache
the same. Next time I won't go empty
or drain myself too soon. How could I have known
the old taste of his mouth would be a thirst
in mine, or come up in my sleep
whispering, *Remember? Remember?*

2.
Seven hour night from New York and up
into the whoosh of jet propulsion,
layer after layer of clouds. Miles below:
the Atlantic. Hours ahead: me.

You ask about my road weary feet, tobacco breath,
and thighs brown and turbulent as the Seine.
Your grey eyes pull me up for air and promise:
"These are my last words on Paris and lost love,
my last journey back."

First sky, then altitude. Suspension
and the angle of descent to home.
We're made different by it, but never safe.

Through the Arc de Triomphe, down the
    Champs Elysees,
cutting mountain fog in Massachusetts to the red
ground in Mali, the chattering sunset in Lagos
or combing traffic below Brooklyn Bridge.
Up cobblestones to the teasing moon above Cannes,
we claw out landmarks etched into our flesh:
your Africa, my Europe, our America.

Believe me. These things happen:

Years from now in a sudden lift
from the runway, one great letting go
of metal and earth, one piercing whirr
of engines to the applause of clouds,
those bits of gravel in the throat
can churn up saying, *You will remember, remember me.*

INTO CAMP GROUND

James Arthur Baldwin
1924-1987

Hungers of the flesh, the timeless terror
of our need, the barter of our liberty for lies,
these were your watchwords and your witness,
the steel of your surrender to our song:

True believer,
I want to cross over
into camp ground.

One fiery still November, not in Harlem,
nor Paris, but in woods up North,
you seared my hands where the rocks cried out,
opening to your deepest room, Giovanni's, and mine.

B L O O D   P O S I T I V E

1. The Children Wonder

What did you do when the thighs of our brothers
were nothing but bruises and bones?
Where did you go when the songs said to march
and you only meandered and minced?
Whom did you kiss with your cough
and elaborate phlegm? How much time
did you borrow on blood?
What was the price of your fear and your fist?

DON'T MOVE.
YOUR MEMORY OR YOUR LIFE.

2. The Dead Speak

Leave us alone.
We did nothing but worship our kind.
When you love as we did you will know
there is no life but this
and history will not be kind.
Now take what you need and get out.

ONE BY ONE

They won't go when I go.
—Stevie Wonder

Live bravely in the hurt of light.
—C.H.R.

The children in the life:
Another telephone call. Another man gone.
How many pages are left in my diary?
Do I have enough pencils? Enough ink?
I count on my fingers and toes the past kisses,
the incubating years, the months ahead.

Thousands. Many thousands
Many thousands gone.

I have no use for numbers beyond this one,
one man, one face, one torso
curled into mine for the ease of sleep.
We love without mercy.
We live bravely in the light.

Thousands. Many thousands.

Chile, I knew he was funny, one of the children,
a member of the church, a friend of Dorothy's.

He knew the Websters pretty well, too.
Girlfriend, he was real.
Remember we used to sit up in my house
pouring tea, dropping beads,
dishing this one and that one?

You got any T-cells left?
The singularity of death. The mounting thousands.
It begins with one and grows by one
and one and one and one
until there's no one left to count.

THE 80'S MIRACLE DIET

Yours free without the asking
Quick delivery via overnight male,
Special Handling, or ten year incubation.
How I Lost 40 Pounds in Two Weeks

Cocktails of Perrier with a twist of AZT,
Bactrim broiled with bacon bits,
Egg lipid quiche for brunch. Our tongues
Ablaze on toast points in a soundless howl.
The most talented minds, the best bodies
Of my generation going up in smoke.

Act now. Dial 1-800-1-GOT-IT-2.
Our operators are standing by.
I have photographs to prove it:
Before and After and Passed Away.

J U S T   U S ,   A T   H O M E

He's back in his baby blanket,
curled fetus-like and thin.

His cough now such a part of speech
it is language between us.

When we touch, our bones clatter and clang,
this new music the only song we sing.

Tommy, the teddy-bear, a friend of forty years,
has not forgotten how to comfort or applaud

Our skeleton dance, our silent screams.

AUNT IDA PIECES A QUILT

You are right, but your patch isn't big enough.
—Jesse Jackson

When a cure is found and the last panel is sewn into
place, the Quilt will be displayed in a permanent home as
a national monument to the individual, irreplaceable
people lost to AIDS—and the people who knew and
loved them most.
—Cleve Jones, founder, The NAMES Project

They brought me some of his clothes. The hospital gown.
Those too-tight dungarees, his blue choir robe
with the gold sash. How that boy could sing!
His favorite color in a necktie. A Sunday shirt.
What I'm gonna do with all this stuff?
I can remember Junie without this business.
My niece Francine say they quilting all over the country.
So many good boys like her boy, gone.

At my age I ain't studying no needle and thread.
My eyes ain't so good now and my fingers lock in a fist,
they so eaten up with arthritis. This old back
dont' take kindly to bending over a frame no more.
Francine say ain't I a mess carrying on like this.
I could make two quilts the time I spend running
    my mouth.

Just cut his name out the cloths, stitch something nice
about him. Something to bring him back. You can do it,
Francine say. Best sewing our family ever had.
Quilting ain't that easy, I say. Never was easy.
Y'all got to help me remember him good.

Most of my quilts was made down South. My Mama
and my Mama's Mama taught me. Popped me on the tail
if I missed a stitch or threw the pattern out of line.
I did "Bright Star" and "Lonesome Square" and "Rally
    Round,"
what many folks don't bother with nowadays. Then
    Elmo and me
married and came North where the cold in Connecticut
cuts you lie a knife. We was warm, though.
We had sackcloth and calico and cotton, 100% pure.
What they got now but polyester-rayon. Factory made.

Let me tell you something. In all my quilts there's a secret
nobody knows. Every last one of them got my name Ida
stitched on the backside in red thread.

That's where Junie got his flair. Don't let nobody fool you.
When he got the Youth Choir standing up and singing
the whole church would rock. He'd throw up his hands
from them wide blue sleeves and the church would hush
right down to the funeral parlor fans whisking the air.
He'd toss his head back and holler and we'd all cry holy.

And nevermind his too-tight dungarees.
I caught him switching down the steet one Saturday
    night,
and I seen him more than once. I said, Junie,
You ain't got to let the world know all your business.
Who cared where he went when he wanted to have fun.
He'd be singing his heart out come Sunday morning.

When Francine say she gonna hang this quilt in the
    church
I like to fall out. A quilt ain't no show piece,

it's to keep you warm. Francine say it can do both.
Now I ain't so old fashioned I can't change,
but I made Francine come over and bring her daughter
Belinda. We cut and tacked his name, *JUNIE*.
Just plain and simple. *"JUNIE, our boy."*
Cut the J in blue, the U in gold. N in dungarees
just as tight as you please. The I from the hospital gown
and the white shirt he wore First Sunday. Belinda
put the necktie E in the cross stitch I showed her.

Wouldn't you know we got to talking about Junie.
We could smell him in the cloth.
Underarm. Afro-Sheen pomade. Gravy stains.
I forgot all about my arthritis.
When Francine left me to finish up, I swear
I heard Junie giggling right along with me
as I stitched Ida on the backside in red thread.

Francine say she gonna send this quilt to Washington
like folks doing from all cross the country,
so many good people gone. Babies, mothers, fathers,
and boys like our Junie. Francine say
they gonna piece this quilt to another one,
another name and another patch
all in a larger quilt getting larger and larger.

Maybe we all like that, patches waiting to be pieced.
Well, I don't know about Washington.
We need Junie here with us. And Maxine,
she cousin May's husband's sister's people,
she having a baby and here comes winter already.
The cold cutting like knives. Now where did I put that
    needle?

L A N D ' S   E N D

PROVINCETOWN

Zero ground, fickle sandbar
where graves and gravity conspire,

Beer bottle amber and liquor green
surrender their killing shards.

Like ashes, dust, even glass
turns back into what it was.

Skeletal driftwood and seaweed hair
beg for a body. Any body.

Yet all you see is surf out there,
simply more and more of nothing.

If you must leave us, now or later,
the sea will bring you back.

HEARTBEATS

Work out. Ten laps.
Chin ups. Look good.

Steam room. Dress warm.
Call home. Fresh air.

Eat right. Rest well.
Sweetheart. Safe sex.

Sore throat. Long flu.
Hard nodes. Beware.

Test blood. Count cells.
Reds thin. Whites low.

Dress warm. Eat well.
Short breath. Fatigue.

Night sweats. Dry cough.
Loose stools. Weight loss.

Get mad. Fight back.
Call home. Rest well.

Don't cry. Take charge.
No sex. Eat right.

Call home. Talk slow.
Chin up. No air.

Arms wide. Nodes hard.
Cough dry. Hold on.

Mouth wide. Drink this.
Breathe in. Breathe out.

No air. Breathe in.
Breathe in. No air.

Black out. White rooms.
Head hot. Feet cold.

No work. Eat right.
CAT scan. Chin up.

Breathe in. Breathe out.
No air. No air.

Thin blood. Sore lungs.
Mouth dry. Mind gone.

Six months? Three weeks?
Can't eat. No air.

Today? Tonight?
It waits. For me.

Sweet heart. Don't stop.
Breathe in. Breathe out.

TURNING FORTY
IN THE 90'S

April 1990

We promised to grow old together, our dream
since years ago when we began
to celebrate our common tenderness
and touch. So here we are:

Dry, ashy skin, falling hair, losing breath
at the top of stairs, forgetting things.
Vials of Septra and AZT line the bedroom dresser
like a boy's toy army poised for attack—
your red, my blue, and the casualties are real.

Now the dimming in your man's eyes and mine.
Our bones ache as the muscles dissolve,
exposing the fragile gates of ribs, our last defense. heart
And we calculate pensions and premiums.
You are not yet forty-five, and I
not yet forty, but neither of us for long.

No Senior discounts here, so we clip coupons
like squirrels in late November, foraging
each remaining month or week, day or hour.
We hold together against the throb and jab
of yet another bone from out of nowhere poking through.
You grip the walker and I hobble with a cane.
 Two witnesses for our bent generation.

THE FALLING SKY

IN MEMORY OF CHESTER WEINERMAN

This lonely hour in autumn, this thick November sky,
Memory hovers above us like the threat of rain
Or razor blades of sun and shooting stars.
I could never catch a baseball, never throw one.
At bat or in the field, I'd chop madly and flail
My windmill arms at the air, at the air,
All under the jeering, brilliant laughter of the blue,
"Easy out. Easy out!"

When at last you knew the sky was falling
You were too sick to go outside, even when lightning
Broke the day into pieces shimmering down.
But in my dream you bolted from the bed.
You ran to us, screaming "Save me. Save me!"
And we held you tight, held onto your visible bones.

Now I, too, have started to thin and sweat and cough.
Once again the low clouds conspire, playground bullies
Their laughter bursting into gloom and gray.
Dust already gathers at the grit line of my teeth.
Ash coats my skin like a uniform with no number.
The wind whirls through the deserted diamond field,
And my hands scramble at the fast falling sky,
And a sudden, unknown voice cries out:
"Come on, catch it. You can do it. Catch it."

A N D   T H E S E   A R E
J U S T   A   F E W   .   .   .

This poem is for the epidemic dead and the living.
  Remember them?
Your neighbors, your siblings, your daughters and
  your sons.

This poem is for Robert, remember Bob? He told me my
  lover's name
Before we had even met. Then he went dancing alone
  until daybreak.

This poem is for Wilbert, remember Will? Who served
  his country
With diplomacy and grace. He showed Africa that we
  all are kin.

This poem is for Joseph, remember Joe? Whose longing
For the language of black men loving black men
  became our lore.

This poem is for Samuel, remember Sam? Who taught
  those who could
Barely read until the skin around his mouth peeled off
  in pages.

This poem is for Joel, remember Joel? A dazzler of
  demography,
A man for numbers, student of the migratory patterns
  of mankind.

This poem is for Gridley, remember Grid? He cried
  when he got sick,
Then left Peru for Wisconsin where he felt safe.
  He died there.

This poem is for Allan, remember Al? Who loved
    theater, and dance.
He worked with homeless teens and returned home
    too thin to twirl.

This poem is for Christopher, remember Chris?
    The Bergdorf windows
He dressed. The color he left behind when he no
    longer could see.

This poem is for Gregory, remember Greg? Going,
    then gone.
Journalist, the print of his legacy read from D.C.
    to Detroit.

This poem is for Chester, remember Chet? Whose
    battered lungs
Left him screaming the purest poetry on empty
    hospital walls.

This poem is for Rita and Eddie. They taught us
    sign language
For love: three fingers teasing the air above a bridge
    of knuckles.

This poem is for Richard, remember Rich? Poised
    with puns
For the quick meter of his mind, for the constancy of
    our embrace.

This poem is for the epidemic living and the dead.
Remember them, remember me.

I'LL BE SOMEWHERE
LISTENING FOR MY NAME

When he calls me, I will answer
When he calls me, I will answer
When he calls me, I will answer
I'll be somewhere listening for my name

I'll be somewhere listening
I'll be somewhere listening
I'll be somewhere listening for my name

As gay men and lesbians, we are the sexual niggers of our society.

Some of you may have never before been treated like second-class, disposable citizen. Some of you have felt a certain privilege and protection in being white, which is not to say that others are accustomed to or have accepted being racial niggers and feel less alienated. Since I have never encountered a person of no color, I assume that we are all persons of color. Like fashion victims, though, we are led to believe that some colors are more acceptable than others, and those acceptable colors have been so endowed with universality and desirability that the color hardly seems to exist at all— except, of course, to those who are of a different color and pushed outside the rainbow. My own fantasy is to be locked inside a Bennetton ad.

No one dares call us sexual niggers, at least not to our faces. But the epithets can be devastating or entertaining: We are faggots and dykes, sissies and bulldaggers. We are funny, sensitive, Miss Thing, friends of Dorothy, or men with "a little sugar in the blood," and we call ourselves what we will. As an anthropologist/linguist friend of mine calls me in one breath, "Miss Lady Sister Woman Honey Girl Child."

Within this environment of sexual and racial nigger-dom, recovery isn't easy. Sometimes it is like trying to fit a size 12 basketball player's foot into one of Imelda Marcos's pumps. The color might be right, but the shoe still pinches. Or, for the more fashionable lesbians in the audience, lacing up those combat boots only to have extra eyelets staring you in the face, and you feel like Olive Oyl gone trucking after Minnie Mouse.

As for me, I've become an acronym queen: BGM ISO same or other. HIV plus or minus. CMV, PCP, MAI, AZT, ddI, ddC. Your prescription gets mine.

Remember those great nocturnal emissions of your adolescent years? They told us we were men, and the gooey stuff proved it. Now in the nineties, our nocturnal emissions are night sweats, inspiring fear, telling us we are mortal and sick, and that time is running out.

In my former neighborhood in Manhattan, I was a member of the 4H Club: the Happy Homosexuals of Hamilton Heights. Now it is the 3D Club: the dead, the dying, those in despair. I used to be in despair; now I'm just dying.

I come to you bearing witness to a broken heart; I come to you bearing witness to a broken body—but a witness to an unbroken spirit. Perhaps it is only to you that such witness can be brought and its jagged edges softened a bit and made meaningful.

We are facing the loss of our entire generation. Lesbians lost to various cancers, gay men lost to AIDS. What kind of witness will you bear? What truthtelling are you brave enough to utter and endure the consequences of your unpopular message?

Last summer my lover Richard died. We had been lovers for twelve years. His illness and death were so much a part of my illness and life that I felt that I too had died. I'm just back from Florida, visiting his family and attending the unveiling of his headstone. Later this month, our attorney will file the necessary papers for the settling of Richard's estate, and I shall return to our summer home in Provincetown without him, but not without the rich memories of our many years there. And he is everywhere inside me listening for his name.

I've lost Richard; I've lost vision in one eye; I've lost the contact of people I thought were friends; I've lost the future tense from my vocabulary; I've lost my libido; and I've lost more weight and appetite than Nutri-System would want to claim.

My life is closing. Oh, I know all the cliches: "We all have to die," and "Everything comes to an end." But when is an ending a closure, and when does closure become a new beginning? Not always. It is not automatic. We have to work at it. If an end is termination, closure involves the will to remember, which gives new life to memory.

As creators, we appear to strike a bargain with the immortality we assume to be inherent in art. Our work exists outside us and will have a life independent of us. Doris Grumbach, in her recent book, *Coming into the End Zone*, reminds us of the life of books: "Let the book make its own way, even through the thick forest of competitors, compelling readers by the force of its words and its vision."

I am reminded of a poignant line from George Whitmore, who struck a Faustian bargain with AIDS: If he wrote about it, perhaps he wouldn't get it. George, as you know, lost that battle, but his books are still with us. His two novels are *The Confessions of Danny Slocum*, and *Nebraska*. His harrowing reporting on AIDS is called *Someone was Here*. And now George is somewhere listening for his name, hearing it among us.

I am not above bargaining for time and health. And I

am troubled by the power of prophecy inherrent in art. One becomes afraid to write because one's wildest speculations may in fact come true. I wrote all the AIDS poems published in Michael Klein's *Poets for Life* before I knew I was HIV positive. I was responding in part to my sense of isolation and helplessness as friends of mine fell ill. And when I published the poem, "And These are Just a Few," in the *Kenyon Review*, I made a point of acknowledging the dead and those yet fighting for life. I'm sorry to report that of the twenty people mentioned in the poem, only two are presently alive.

As writers, we are a curious lot. We begin our projects with much apprehension about the blank page. But then as the material assumes its life, we resist writing that last stanza or paragraph. We want to avoid putting a final period to it all. Readers are no better. We all want to know what new adventures await Huck Finn or if Ishmael finally "comes out" following his "marriage" with QueeQueg. As sequels go, I'm not sure the world needed Ripley's extension to *Gone with the Wind*, but consider *Rocky 10*, in which the son of the erstwhile fighter discovers he is gay and must take on the arch villain Harry Homophobia. Would the title have to be changed to *Rockette?*

Then there is the chilling threat of erasure. Gregory, a friend and former student of mine, died last fall. On the day following a memorial service for him, we all were having lunch and laughing over our fond memories of Greg and his many accomplishments as a journalist. Suddenly his lover had a shock. He had forgotten the remaining copies of the memorial program in the rental car he had just returned. Frantic to retrieve the programs, which had Greg's picture on the cover and reprints of his autobiographical essays inside, his lover called the rental agency to reclaim the material.

They had already claimed the car, but he could come out there, they said, and dig through the dumpster for whatever he could find. Hours later, the lover returned empty-handed, the paper programs already shredded, burned, and the refuse carted away. Greg had been cremated once again, but this time without remains or a classy urn to house them. The image of Greg's lover sifting through the dumpster is more haunting than the reality of Greg's death, for Greg had made his peace with the world. The world, however, had not made its peace with him.

His siblings refused to be named in one very prominent obituary, and Greg's gayness and death from AIDS were not to be mentioned at the memorial service. Fortunately few of us heeded the family's prohibition. While his family and society may have wanted to dispose of Greg even after his death, some of us tried to reclaim him and love him again and only then release him.

I was reminded of how vulnerable we are as gay men, as black gay men, to the disposal or erasure of our lives.

But Greg was a writer, a journalist who had written on AIDS, on the business world, and on his own curious life journey from his birth in the poor Anacostia district of Washington, DC, to scholarships that allowed him to attend Exeter and then Williams College and on to the city desks of our nations most prominent newspapers. His words are still with us even if his body and those gorgeous programs are gone. And Greg is somewhere listening for his name.

We must, however, guard against the erasure of our experience and our lives. As white gays become more and more prominent—and acceptable to mainstream society—they project a racially exclusive image of gay reality. Few men of color will ever be found on the covers of the *Advocate* or *New York Native*. As white gays deny multiculturalism among gays, so too do black communities deny multisexualism among its members. Against this double cremation, we must leave the legacy of our writing and our perspectives on gay and straight experiences.

Our voice is our weapon.

Several months ago the editors of *Lambda Book Report* solicited comments from several of us about the future of gay and lesbian publishing. My comments began by acknowledging my grief for writers who had died before they could make a significant contribution to the literature. The editors said my comments suggested a "bleak and nonexistent future" for gay publishing. Although I still find it difficult to imagine a glorious future for gay publishing, that does not mean I cannot offer some concrete suggestion to ensure that a future does exist.

First, reaffirm the importance of cultural diversity in our community. Second, preserve our literary heritage by posthumous publications and reprints, and third, establish grants and fellowships to ensure that our literary history is written and passed on to others. I don't think these comments are bleak, but they should remind us of one thing: We alone are responsible for the preservation and future of our literature.

If we don't buy our books, they won't get published. If we don't talk about our books, they won't get reviewed. If we don't write our books, they won't get written.

As for me ... I may not be well enough or alive next year to attend the lesbian and gay writers conference, but I'll be somewhere listening for my name.

I may not be around to celebrate with you the

publication of gay literary history. But I'll be somewhere listening for my name.

If I don't make it to Tea Dance in Provincetown or the Pines, I'll be somewhere listening for my name.

You, then, are charged by the possibility of your good health, by the broadness of your vision, to remember us.

This is an adaptation of a keynote speech delivered at OutWrite '92.